sundance publishing

LITTLE RED READERS

Things I Do with My Friends

PETER SLOAN & SHERYL SLOAN

I walk
with my friends.

I run
with my friends.

I swim
with my friends.

I ride
with my friends.

I skip
with my friends.

I skate
with my friends.

I climb
with my friends.

8